STRESS-BUSTER WORKBOOK FOR KIDS

40+ *Fun Activities and Exercises to Manage Emotions, Building Self-Regulation Skills, and Develop Positive Thinking*

By

D. Erickson

Climax Publishers

Legal Notice

This book is copyright protected. It is only to be used for personal purposes. Without the author's or publisher's permission, you cannot paraphrase, quote, copy, distribute, sell, or change any part of the information in this book.

Disclaimer Notice

This book is written and published independently. Please keep in mind that the material in this publication is solely for educational and entertaining purposes. All efforts have provided authentic, up-to-date, trustworthy, and comprehensive information. There are no express or implied assurances. The purpose of this book's material is to assist readers in having a better understanding of the subject matter. The activities, information, and exercises are provided solely for self-help information. This book is not intended to replace expert psychologists, legal, financial, or other guidance. If you require counseling, please get in touch with a qualified professional.

By reading this text, the reader accepts that the author will not be held liable for any damages, indirectly or directly, experienced due to the information included herein, particularly, but not limited to, omissions, errors, or inaccuracies. You are accountable for your decisions, actions, and consequences as a reader.

About the Author

D. Erickson is a child psychologist and writer. He has five years of experience and knowledge in dealing with children combating stress, anxiety and other psychological issues. He has worked with hundreds of children and led them towards a healthy and happy lifestyle. He has developed this "Stress Buster Workbook for Kids" with effective and entertaining activities, exercises and strategies.

Table of Contents

Introduction

Unsurprisingly, stress affects kids. Our kids face various difficulties now and will continue to do so in the future, from academic and social demands to outside factors like growing up during a war or even a global epidemic.

According to a US WebMD poll, children exhibit negative behaviors associated with stress in 72% of cases, and 62% of those cases include physical symptoms like headaches and stomachaches.

Then how can you tell if your children are under stress? What signs of stress do children show? What can you do to help them?

But for that, you need to understand what stress really is.

Stress frequently occurs when we are under pressure. A little bit of stress may help and motivate us to accomplish our goals. However, stress that feels out of control can impact our emotions, health, and interpersonal connections. Some people develop burnout, which is a state of complete physical and emotional exhaustion, after experiencing prolonged stress. Thankfully, there are ways to stop stress from getting out of hand.

Any event that requires the kid to adapt or adjust might generate stress in youngsters. Stress may sometimes result from positive changes, like starting a new interest, although it is more common when something negative happens, like being sick or losing a family member. You may help them by attempting to recognize signs of stress and teaching your child effective coping skills. A negative life change may cause a child's stress to increase.

Your body produces stress-related chemicals, including cortisol and adrenaline. These chemicals, which shield the body from quick action, sometimes known as "fight or flight," have a number of detrimental effects. Some of the negative effects are anxiety, sadness, difficulties in concentrating, dizziness, weight gain or loss, and sleep issues. These negative impacts further raise stress level, which only makes the situation worse. You must learn how to help your children deal with stress when it happens.

The book is focused on helping your child learn to manage stress before it disrupts their personality and behavior. It contains more than interactive and fun activities and exercises to alleviate stress and engage your kids in their spare time productively.

The book has five sections, where the first section will provide you with the foundational knowledge for teaching your kids about stress. It will include stories to elaborate on concepts like psychology and symptoms of stress. Moreover, it will contain stress management strategies and tips for children.

The next three sections will provide exciting exercises and worksheets on emotions, negative thoughts and self-regulation. The last part will offer additional strategies and advice on lifestyle and emotional changes for a stress-free life.

How do I know all of this?

I am a child psychologist with five years of experience and knowledge in this field. I deal with children of all ages suffering from stress, anxiety and other psychological issues. I have worked with hundreds of kids and directed them towards a happy and healthy lifestyle. The activities and exercises I have mentioned in this book are all effective and proven to give results.

Before we move on to the first chapter, I would like to have a few words with you and your child!

Let's get started.

Dear Parents,

I have been working directly with children for more than five years and have seen younger children get more stressed. Early in my work, due to a physical condition or other contextual factors, the smallest children who came into my office needed social skills instruction or support (due to parents' divorce, loss, parent suffering from cancer). Today, children as young as five come to me for assistance in controlling the overwhelming stress and worry they experience regularly. Over the course of my work, a lot has changed for young children, and I believe that children and parents alike more than ever now need encouragement and stress-management techniques.

At the moment, parents' most frequent query to me is, "How can I train my child to handle stress and obstacles?" The expectation gap (the difference between what parents believe their children are capable of and what they are developmentally prepared for) appears to widen quickly, causing more stress. This gap can be attributed to academics that are above a child's developmental level, almost constant testing, and the expectation that children specialize in a sport or other activity by the beginning of elementary school. Modern youth encounter challenges that sometimes seem insurmountable, from bullying (even in kindergarten) and peer pressure to catastrophic catastrophes, school shootings, and COVID-19.

How can we resolve each of these problems? By demonstrating to children how to withstand unpleasant feelings and deal with stress when it arises. The Stress-Buster Workbook for Kids fills that need. This book will teach children aged four to eleven how to deal with pressures and bad emotions by using activities and scripts that I created and tested with children over the last five years.

The Stress-Buster Workbook for Kids is the ideal resource for parents, teachers, therapists, and other professionals dealing with young children. It is designed to give a variety of solutions since we know that every child is unique and needs tactics that work for them. Kids who are stressed can quickly find respite from the exercises because of their simplicity and effectiveness.

With this book, I hope you will be able to support your young loved ones more effectively. Even if we are not all in the same boat every day, we may raft up to support one another as we navigate tough waters. Consider this my gift to you as a life jacket. It will act as a little flotation device to keep you above the water during choppy waters.

Dear Kids,

This book is for you! Recently, I have seen that youngsters are under a lot of stress. Perhaps school is too challenging, sports are overly competitive or making and retaining friends is more difficult than you anticipated. These are only a few reasons, but young people, just like you, tell me all kinds of other explanations. I want you to understand that going through stress is a normal part of growing up. Everybody can learn how to handle stress since everyone experiences stress from time to time.

This book will show you how to recognize your own signs of stress and figure out what to do to feel better, as well as how to get past frustrating situations (because, let's face it, we all run into them!), communicate your needs and feelings to others, believe in yourself, and use positive thinking to get through challenging situations. That may seem like a lot, but I have faith in your ability to do it.

This book can be read in stages or all at once. After reading this book, you will be an authority on stress and know everything there is to know about managing it. You will even be able to educate other kids and even your grownups!

It is crucial for you to realize that you are not alone, even if feeling worried may occasionally make you feel lonely. I hope that knowing how to manage your stress makes you feel more self-assured and content.

All About Me

Before starting our stress-buster journey, introduce yourself.

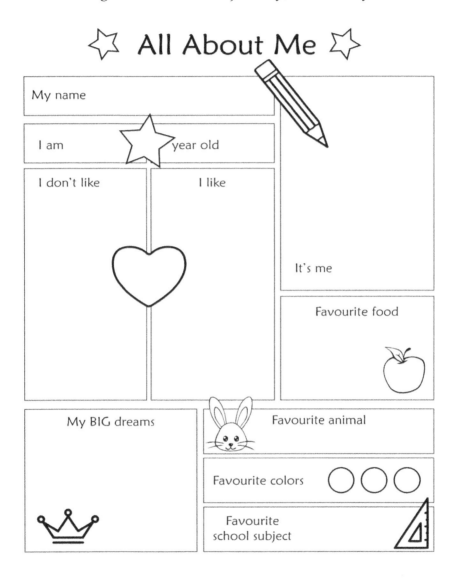

☆ **All About Me** ☆

My name

I am _____ year old

I don't like | I like

It's me

Favourite food

My BIG dreams

Favourite animal

Favourite colors

Favourite school subject

Chapter 1: ABC of Stress Management

Do you know the story about the Wise King?

A wise king was once troubled all the time about something. He used to have occasional feelings of helplessness and misfortune for a variety of causes. He frequently took on the persona of one of those simple people who, due to a lack of resources, could never tackle an issue in an imaginative and courageous manner. He never laughed again for the rest of his life as a result. Even his ministers never saw him laughing. Even they never smiled in the King's presence.

The King's well-wishers secretly thought of ways to change his outlook on life in the future. They thus came up with a plan for the next time the King's court was gathered. Like every previous time, the King called for his closest minister, saying, "I'm worried about something."

"Yes, Your Honor," swiftly said the minister ", I am aware of it and have given it some thought." "How can you know of my fear even when I have not told you anything about it," said the surprised King. The minister gave a humble reply, "I am not interested in knowing more about your issue since I already have a solution, Your Majesty." This shocked the King, who questioned, "How can you know the solution even without understanding my problem?" Minister replied, "You could have more than one problem, Your Majesty, but there is only one solution to them all."

The King was confused and said, "May I know what is the solution to my problem?" The minister said, "Your Majesty, please do not worry about the solution." "Well, how can I not worry if there is a problem," the minister said, and the King struggled to understand what he meant.

"Has your stress alleviated any of your problems, Your Majesty?" Minister politely enquired. The King said, "No." "Well, why worry if that is the case?" The key to success is "not worrying." Worrying only makes matter worse. The joy of life is found in rejoicing, not in stress. Your Majesty, you are quite knowledgeable. You guide us with your knowledge. So why do not you stand next to us while projecting a more vibrant picture of yourself?"

The King finally realized his mistake. Additionally, he realized how gently his pastor and well-wishers had imparted this important life lesson upon him. When he started to laugh, he was surprised to hear everyone else laugh as well.

This old story teaches us that fretting does not assist us in resolving our issues. Instead, it makes us weaker and gets in the way of our success. If you are able to get rid of your worry, you have already won half the battle.

Let me help you understand the stress and worrying better.

1.1 Inside My Brain and Body

When something makes you uncomfortable, you experience stress. Your brain instantly activates a physical and mental alarm system known as stress whenever it recognizes a potential threat. Here's how it functions.

Say you are about to cross the street. You suddenly notice a vehicle speeding around the corner. Stress chemicals in your body cause you to respond rapidly. You get an extra boost of energy, attention, strength, and speed, thanks to stress hormones. You widen your eyes. Your brain is more alert. Your attention is focused. Your heart beats more quickly to ensure more oxygen to your muscles. Your breathing quickens. You avoid the automobile and jump back to safety, thanks to your body's stress alarm. Whew!

Your brain switches off the stress alarm when you are secure. The stress hormones are turned off by your body. Your body recovers to its natural, unstressed state once the stress chemicals cease flowing. Both your body and mind relax. You cautiously cross the street after checking both sides.

The fight-flight-or-freeze response is another name for your body's stress alarm. That is because stress gets you ready to fight more fiercely, flee more quickly, or freeze in place if necessary.

"So is Stress Good for Me?"

It depends. Let me explain.

Our stress reaction has its earliest roots in ancient times. Imagine squaring off against a saber-toothed cat as one of our distant ancestors. Your brain orders your body to do things it might not typically be able to accomplish, like running faster to get away from the attacker, as you become aware of the risk. The brain stimulates a number of glands, which then release a flood of hormones that have a profound impact on your body. Like I told you, we call it the "fight or flight" reaction.

Modern short-term stressors are usually quite different from wild predators; more frequently, we encounter environmental and psychological stresses like tough competition or deadlines, significant life changes, or feeling uncomfortable in a particular circumstance. However, your body responds by turning on the same systems using the same ancient toolkit. The stress reaction can be advantageous, just as it gave our ancestors that additional edge to escape a predator. Perhaps it inspires you to persevere and finish a marathon or improves your academic achievement. It is also crucial to realize that various persons might experience the same stressor at varying intensities. How each of us experiences the challenge of a stressful circumstance depends on a variety of factors, including life experience and brain chemistry.

Once the perceived threat (or deadline or life event) has passed, and your body has regained balance, the stress reaction often fades away. However, the stress response remains in a state of alertness heightened when a danger persists over time. The body crumbles when the nervous system is constantly activated due to the "stress reaction."

Imagine you are running away from a deadly tiger. How do you feel?

Now, how about you felt like that all day long all week? Your brain and body would slowly give up and stop working.

Long-term stress can have negative psychological and physical effects, e.g. your immune system and cardiovascular system may weaken, and your risk of anxiety or depression rises.

Why am I Stressed?

There are many things that might stress you out, both good and bad stress. Good or frequent tension may become apparent when you are called on in class or have to submit a report. Have you ever had hand sweats or stomach flutters? That may be a healthy indicator of stress, encouraging you to complete your tasks. For instance, you could succeed if your anxiety drives you to plan carefully before reading your book report to the class.

Negative stress, however, might result if the stressed sensations last for an extended period of time. You cannot feel good if your family is bickering, a family member is ill, you are having problems in school, or you are dealing with anything that makes you unhappy every day. You would not benefit from stress, and it can even make you ill.

Here are some ideas to help you figure out the reason why you are stressed.

- **School**

    Many kids experience pressure to do well in school. And for some, the amount of material they must study during the day and the homework they must complete at night might feel daunting. Youngsters may get worried if they get behind on their homework. It may frequently imply that they are too busy to play or engage in other enjoyable things.

- **Peer Pressure**

  It can be challenging for kids to make friends, and

  many of them experience peer pressure. This can sometimes lead to people acting in ways they may not feel confident or at ease.

- **Exams**

  Test pressure may affect adolescents and teens. According to Childline, a counselling service for children and young people between the ages of 12 and 15 were most likely to seek assistance for exam stress. Fear of failing and the desire to avoid disappointing their parents were two of the most prevalent worries. People who called Childline, as a result, claimed that the stress of the exams was causing them to experience sadness, anxiety, panic attacks, and low self-esteem.

- **Bullying**

  Over one million young people are impacted by bullying each year, according to the nonprofit Young Minds. There are a few indications that can indicate a child is experiencing bullying issues. These include being anxious and reclusive, performing poorly in class, making up an illness to avoid going to school, not eating or sleeping well, suffering from strange wounds like bruises, and misplacing their stuff.

- **Changes or Challenges in The Family**

A kid or adolescent may exhibit indications of stress due to family troubles and changes to the norm, such as relocating to a new home or parents divorcing.

- **Global Events**

  These days, it is hard to shield youngsters from terrible news about events like war, natural catastrophes, and terrorist atrocities. As a result, some kids could be concerned for their own safety as well as the safety of their parents, relatives, and friends.

Please have a discussion with your parents and they will help you out in pointing out the root issue of you being stressed out.

1.2 What Stress Looks and Feels Like

Children may display stress in ways that are unexpected since they are miniature adults. Here are a few signs that kids could be under stress or could use extra support:

- **Emotional Outbursts or an Increase in Irritation**

  Stress amplifies sentiments of rage and irritation. There is a chance that kids will act out emotionally in ways that do not fit with either their usual conduct or the circumstances.

- **Difficulty Sleeping**

  Worries and concerns appear to surface around nighttime. Stressed-out kids may have problems sleeping or staying asleep or develop nightmares.

- **Social Withdrawal**

  Stressed-out kids may want to spend more time alone and avoid interacting with friends and relatives.

- **Struggles in the Classroom**

  Stress may be indicated by significant changes in your children's academic performance. Children who are stressed may find it harder to concentrate throughout the school day or when doing their homework. Trouble with friends and classmates might result from emotional outbursts and rage at school.

- **Regular Stomachaches or Headaches**

  Children's bodies emit the stress hormone cortisol into the blood when they are worried or nervous. Headaches and cramping in the abdomen may result from this.

- **Greater Resistance**

  Stressed children could feel irate or overwhelmed. They are trying to find a way to leave their difficult predicament. This may result in rebellious and obstinate actions.

  Remember that a child's stress indicators might change depending on their age, personality, and coping mechanisms. The point is to keep an eye out for sudden or extreme deviations from children's usual conduct.

A child might understand now where his irritable feelings or distant behavior come from!

1.3 My Stress Toolkit

Thousands of years ago, there was a mighty King. With all of his wealth and comforts, this King ought to have been content with his lot in life. But this was not the case! Why he never seemed content with his existence always baffled the King.

He attended upscale meals and parties and grabbed everyone's attention wherever he went, but he could not place what he felt was lacking.

One day, the King rose earlier than usual to explore his palace. He entered his enormous living room and stopped when he heard someone singing happily.

After this song, he heard one of the servants singing, his face beaming with joy.

The King became intrigued by this and extended an invitation to see him in his chambers.

The guy went to the King's chamber as instructed. The King asked him why he was so happy.

The man's reaction to this was as follows: "Your Majesty, I am nothing more than a servant, yet I earn enough money to provide for my family. We do not need much; all we need is a roof over our heads and warm food to eat. My wife and kids, who are happy with whatever little I bring home, serve as my inspiration. My family and I are happy, so I am too."

The King invited his secretary to his office.

The King's anguish was evident. He questioned why a king who could get everything he desired with the snap of his fingers was not pleased while his servant, who had little, was so much happy.

The secretary carefully considered what was being said before responding. "I guess the servant has not been allowed to the 99 clubs, Your Majesty," he retorted.

"What does 99 Club mean? And what is it?" The King was interested.

The helper said, "Your Majesty, you must do the following in order to fully understand what the 99 club is."

"If you put 99 gold pieces in a bag and leave it on this servant's doorway, you will know what the 99 club is."

The King ordered to put 99 gold pieces in the entryway bag of the servant. He was a little nervous and thought he should have put 100 gold pieces in the bag, but he did it because his secretary told him to.

The servant saw a bag on his door. When he opened the bag, he cried with joy. He was in shock at what he saw.

Then, after dropping the bag off at a table, he started counting the coins. He continued to count the money after realizing there were 99 of them, which he thought was an odd number. Each time, however, he came up with the same figure: 99 gold coins.

He pondered what may have happened to the last coin. After all, no one would leave 99 coins. He spent hours searching every inch of his home and grounds in an effort not to lose that one coin. Weary at last, he thought he needed to work harder to make up for that one coin.

Unaware that he had spent the previous night thinking of methods to make enough money to buy that gold coin, he woke up in a terrible mood the next morning, cursing at his children and wife. He arrived at work as usual but not in his customary upbeat mood, singing joyfully, as he had been doing his usual errands with a sour disposition.

The man's abrupt attitude change puzzled the King. He called his secretary into his office immediately. The King's secretary once again listened as the King addressed the servant. Even though the servant ought to have been thrilled after receiving the gold coins, the monarch couldn't believe that the servant, who had been singing and content with his life up until yesterday, had suddenly changed his attitude.

The secretary replied modestly, "Goodness gracious! The servant has joined the 99 Club. People who have everything but are never content are known as members of the "99 club, and they constantly try to add just one more to reach the magic number of 100!

We have a lot we should be thankful for and can get by very little, but when we are given something better and greater, we want it even more! We are no longer the contented and happy individuals we once were because we constantly desire more and fail to appreciate the cost involved. We sacrifice sleep and happiness as a necessary cost of meeting our growing needs and objectives, damaging those around us. When you join the 99 clubs, it's all about it."

When the King heard this, he made the decision to stop worrying about rounding off big to bigger. He decided to move forward and enjoy all of life's tiny joys.

Let's help you find your joy!

Strategies and Tips

I have put together a few suggestions to help you manage stress:

- **Change Attitude**

  Change your perspective from "stress hurts" to "stress helps". If you realize that stressful situations will not persist forever, stress can serve as a catalyst for progress. Instead, these circumstances serve as obstacles to be conquered and lessons to be learned.

  The brain rewires itself to recall and learn from the event following a significant stress reaction. The brain does this to prepare you for similar stressful future circumstances.

  The brain releases the chemical noradrenaline in response to stress. Too much noradrenaline impairs the brain's ability to function at its best. But guess what? Low noradrenaline is not good either.

  According to Robertson, somewhat modest amounts of stress can strengthen brain function, making people smarter and happier.

  Here are a few steps to change your perspective about stress:

  - Develop a "stress help" mentality for yourself. Recognize that you cannot avoid stress, that certain stress might be good for you, and that stress can be a chance to develop.

> - Rather than brushing off your stress, try to understand what is causing it. You should know: Life is certain to be stressful at times.

> - Stress comes and goes.

> - If you pause and take the time to learn from stressful situations, act and look for answers, stressful events may be useful. Give examples based on your personal experiences.

- Identify growth opportunities or lessons that might be drawn from your most recent difficulty.

> - Recall any tense circumstances from the past. What lessons did you draw from such encounters?

> - What strengths did you rely upon to deal with these circumstances?

> - What strengths do you now have?

You will have a much healthier connection with stress and find it simpler to manage if it is seen as a chance for growth.

- **Teach Yourself to Avoid the Worst Case Scenario Thinking**

  Children, as well as adults frequently think catastrophically while being under stress. "My life is ruined if I fail this test," or "Kate isn't treating me well. No one will ever like me."

  Start by acknowledging your feelings when this happens.

  Use the "worst-case scenario exercise" after that. "What could possibly go wrong?" ask yourself. "What is the worst that may happen if Kate continues to be cruel or if your child actually fails the test?"

  You may also inquire about the likelihood of this scenario occurring and whether there are any alternative situations that are more likely to occur. Continue by asking, "What would you do if that did happen?" and, if necessary, work with your parents to brainstorm a solution.

  You will feel more in control of your tension if you come up with an achievable solution. Once you have a strategy in place for the worst-case situation, you will also worry less.

- **Move from a Fixed to Growth Mindset**

  You will need to change from a fixed attitude to a growth mindset in order to reframe stress. According to studies, even a quick growth mindset approach may drastically lower stress and boost a kid's grades.

When faced with difficult circumstances, we frequently feel overwhelmed and are more prone to adopt a fixed mindset: there is nothing we can do to improve the situation, our options are restricted, and so we should probably give up.

Let's say you are worried about a test. You believe that studying more would not help. "I will fail at the exam no matter what I would. It is hopeless."

You can adopt a growth mentality by pointing out that the situation is not final, that it can be changed, and that they do have some control over it.

Help yourself find a growth mindset alternative if you find yourself saying a fixed mindset statement, such as "I can't do this" or "I'm just not good at math."

Remind yourself that working and trying many solutions can help you solve the problem, lessen you tension, and encourage you to use growth mindset affirmations.

- **Learn Problem-Solving**

  After adopting a growth mindset and reframing stress, you need to learn how to put these concepts into reality through solving problems. Before this actually takes hold, there will probably be a lot of examples, modelling, and practical experience required.

  Below are the following three steps as an excellent place to start:

Emotion naming and validation is the first step. When you name your feelings, such as overwhelmed, concerned, or nervous, validate how you feel.

Go to a calming area. It might be wise to make one if you do not already have one. So you are prepared to solve problems, learn, and grow, allowing yourself to process your emotions and relax your body. You can deep breathe or use growth mindset affirmations such as, "If I try, I can perform well on this test."

Solve the issue! Work with your parents, come up with possible answers while listening more than you speak. Some examples may be studying with a friend who is succeeding in the class, asking the teacher for additional assistance, or allocating a specific amount of time each day to studying.

After coming up with various ideas, weigh the advantages and disadvantages of each one before letting them select.

You will have a number of backup plans available in case the main plan (let's call it Plan A) fails. Your problem will become a lot less stressful once you realize this. Additionally, after you have mastered the discipline of problem-solving, you will be equipped to handle challenging circumstances on your own.

The next section is special. I need you do something for me. Find a time that your parents are free and read aloud the following section for them! It will help you build better understanding with each other and spend quality time together. Yay! Time for a fun activity.

- "Pay attention to your kid. Ask your youngster to describe the issue. Keep your composure and listen with curiosity, patience, openness, and care. Resist the desire to criticize, scold, judge, or suggest what your child should have done instead. The goal is to listen to your child's worries and feelings. By asking questions like "And then what happened?" you might try to acquire the complete narrative. Give it some time. Allow your youngster to take their time as well.

- Say it aloud. When you see that anything is upsetting your kid, let them know. Name the emotion you believe your child is going through if you can. "It appears that you are still upset about what happened at the playground." It should not be an accusation like, "What happened, then? Are you still mad about that? ") or put a child in the spot. The fact that you are curious to learn more about your child's worry is merely a casual observation. Be understanding and kind, and show you want to understand.

- Briefly describe the emotions you believe your child was going through. Things like "That must have been distressing," "No surprise you felt angry when they wouldn't let you in the game," or "That must have appeared unfair to you" are examples. Doing this demonstrates your empathy and understanding of your child's feelings. Being heard and understood is crucial for your child to feel supported by you, which is crucial in stressful situations.

- Give it a label. Many younger children still lack the language to express their emotions. Use such terms to teach your child to name the feelings if they appear to be angry or upset. Children who express their emotions verbally learn to communicate and become emotionally aware or able to identify their own emotional states. Children who are capable of doing this are less likely to experience the behavioral boiling point, in which intense emotions are expressed via actions rather than verbal communication.

- After listening, move on. Sometimes all it takes to assist a child's frustrations in starting to melt away is to communicate, listen, and feel understood. Try shifting the subject and going on to something more uplifting and calming after that. Encourage your youngster to come up with a way to feel better. Do not focus on the issue more than it needs.

- If the issue does not require you to move on, come up with ideas. Discuss solutions as a team if a specific issue is causing stress. Encourage your youngster to come up with a few suggestions. If required, you can begin the brainstorming, but do not take on the entire task. By actively participating, your youngster will gain confidence. Support the good suggestions and make necessary additions. How do you think this will work, please?

- Just be there. Children do not always want to talk about their problems. That is okay at times. Tell your children that you will be available for them if they want to chat. Children typically do not want their parents to leave them alone, even when they do not want to converse. Simply being present, giving your child company, and spending time with them might make them feel better. Initiate something you can do together if you sense that your youngster is depressed, anxious or having a difficult day but doesn't feel like talking. Go for a stroll, watch a film, play basketball, or bake cookies. Isn't it comforting to realize how important your presence is?

- Minimize stress. Look for methods to modify the circumstances if they are creating tension. For instance, it can be important to limit activities to ensure that students have the time and energy for their schoolwork if too many after-school activities frequently induce stress.

- Be patient. It hurts as a parent to witness your child experiencing stress or sadness. However, try to restrain your need to solve every issue. Instead, concentrate on encouraging your child to develop problem-solving skills throughout time. This will result in a youngster who can handle life's ups and downs, express emotions, control their emotions when necessary, and bounce back to try something new."

Now, let's hop on to the fun activities and exercises to shoo away stress.

Chapter 2: Develop Emotional Intelligence

Children are not born with the skill to manage their emotions. This ability is not innate in humans. Some children have trouble controlling their emotions because of their temperament or personality type. Children may learn the abilities necessary to develop emotional intelligence throughout time with their parents' aid, including learning how to regulate their emotions.

The relevance of emotional intelligence sometimes takes a backseat in a world that is so centered on academic knowledge. Effectively managing and expressing emotions is not taught to children. They all develop into adults who struggle to manage emotional stress in their personal and professional lives.

A child's capacity for self-regulation enables him or her to control their emotions and act in a way that is acceptable for the circumstances. We have an outburst out of irritation because we can control our emotions and remain cool and collected in spite of distressing situations. Children may learn and practice emotion management just like any other skill when emotional intelligence is taught to them. Remember that controlling one's emotions does not mean steering clear of circumstances that your youngster could find difficult. It involves assisting your youngster in maintaining composure and behaving appropriately even while experiencing uncomfortable feelings.

Do you need to know why it is important to manage your emotions? I have an interesting story for you!

Rick was a little child who was always irritated by everything around him. He was usually fighting with the other kids at school. His teachers were powerless to appease the child. And his classmates' parents were becoming anxious.

The youngster was quickly becoming well-known.

Rick's mother tried all she could to calm Rick down after speaking with school officials. She experimented with several techniques until one day. She returned home with a canvas and paint.

"What is this?" Rick inquired.

"Whenever you feel furious, paint whatever it is you're angry about instead of lashing out," Rick's mother stated as she handed him the painting supplies.

Rick was not thrilled, but he gave it a chance anyhow. Several artworks were done by the little youngster over the next few weeks. They did, however, typically convey unpleasant imagery. So his mother took all the paintings and summoned Rick to discuss them.

"Rick, tell me. "What are the themes of these paintings?"

"Well, the first painting depicts several of the youngsters flaunting their new clothes and electronics. The following artwork is about my teacher, who always tells me how I am doing things incorrectly. The final picture depicts how one of my classmates' fathers urged that I adjust my attitude. All of them irritate me."

Rick's mother took him by the hand and said calmly, "Don't you see it, Rick?"

"See what I mean?"

"You're so upset about all of this, but you've never tried to figure out why you're so angry." "What exactly have all these individuals done to you?"

Rick considered it. It gradually dawned on him that all the individuals he was upset with had done nothing wrong. The students at school were bragging about their wealth, but they never made fun of him for being poor. It wasn't their fault they were wealthier than him.

His instructor could have punished him, but his attitude was clearly causing problems in class. And his schoolmate's father was merely attempting to assist him in correcting his errors.

He never attempted to express his feelings to these folks. He knew his mother had hit every nail on the head.

"Mom, I see it now. I was allowing my bad temper to govern me rather than the other way around."

"You're correct, son. You should work on managing your anger before it swallows you. You're no longer a tiny boy. You should have learned your lesson by now."

Rick agreed with a nod. "Next time you become furious, take a big breath and walk away for a few seconds," his mother said. When you return, talk to the individual you are upset with. You might be astonished to learn that all they want to do is to help you grow as a person.

Rick followed his mother's counsel and began to scrutinize his activities. It took some time, but Rick ultimately grew less irritated over trivial matters. He even began to feel happy when he was with other youngsters.

The Story's Moral:

Don't let your rage rule you. Instead, try to regulate your anger by recognizing where it is coming from and discussing your thoughts with others.

Anger has the ability to overcome us. If you have a terrible temper, you are likely to take it out on someone because you are overthinking the scenario. That is bad news for everyone involved.

That is why it is critical to understand how to manage your anger. And, while everyone has their own style of dealing with anger, the following short stories may give you some ideas on how to channel your bad emotions into something positive so that you do not feel so down.

Dear kids, it is the same for every emotion. If you do not handle it, it makes you lose control of yourself. Stress is an undeniable part of this.

Activity: My Feelings

Identify the emotions that you feel during a stressful event and color them.

Activity: Emotional Stages

Now, here is a list of emotions. Can you write down some situations from your life you can think of, related to these emotions?

Write 2 things or situations that make you feel each of the emotions listed below.

Furious

1. _____

2. _____

Angry

1. _____

2. _____

Frustrated

1. _____

2. _____

Calm

1. _____

2. _____

Activity: Emotions and Actions

There is a strong connection between our emotions and actions. Whenever we feel an emotion, we base our behavior on it. In the previous activity, I gave you an emotional list. This time write emotions by yourself and then note down your actions related to the emotion.

EMOTIONS	ACTIONS

Activity: Anxiety Breakdown

Stress and anxiety are interlinked. When we feel stressed, it can cause anxiety. To see if you are stressed or anxious, this anxiety breakdown sheet will help you. Answer the questions below:

ANXIETY BREAKDOWN

What is making me feel anxious?

What are some of the negative thoughts that I am having?

How is my body responding?

What is the worst thing that can happen?

What do I have in my control to keep this from happening?

What can I do to calm my body down?

What are positive thoughts to help calm my mind?

Activity: What's Okay

Write down thoughts and emotions that are "okay" in a given environment.

Activity: Things That Cause Me Stress

Fill up the shapes with things that cause you stress.

What are the thing that cause me stress?

In each oval, add something that is a stressor to you.

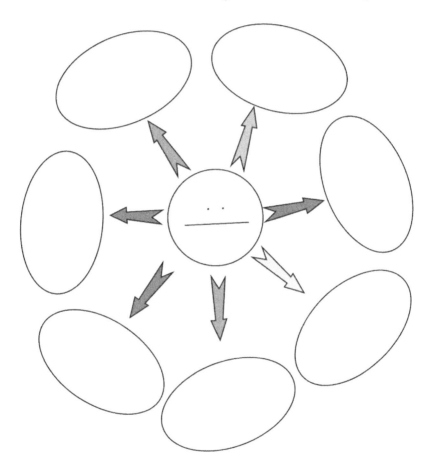

Activity: My Stressed-Out List

Now find out your stressors in the given spaces.

My Stressed - Out list!

Write down all the things that are stressing you out in all the different areas of your life.

School

Family

Friends

Other

What are some helpful things you can do to cope with your stress?

Activity: When I am Feeling Stressed

Write down things you can and should not do while you feel stressed.

When I'm Feeling Stressed

I Can.......      I Should Not.......

Activity: Emotions Daily Check-In

Rate your day out of 10, you have little, no, and too much stress. Draw or write the emotion in the given column. An example is given. This activity will help you keep an eye on your daily stress levels to handle them.

DAY	EMOTIONS	STRESS RATING (10 is the extreme point)
Monday	Frustrated	7/10

Mindfulness Activities to Regulate Emotions

You might be familiar with the mindfulness concept. Helping people live in the moment is the main goal of Mindfulness. This mindset is simpler to control your emotions and improve your relationships.

Mindfulness has been proven to be extremely effective for various issues. Stress, anxiety, depression, and mood disorders are a few of them. However, it is beneficial for almost everyone since it places a strong emphasis on peace of mind.

Mindfulness for Kids

Paying attention to what is going on both around and inside you is mindfulness.

Being mindful involves paying attention to how your body feels as well as to what you see, hear, smell, and taste. You could even experience emotions physically, like a tightness or positive sensation.

Being mindful includes being aware of what your mind is doing.

What happens when you start to be aware of your experiences?

Your ability to concentrate and focus increase when you pay close attention to what is going on around you, helping you be better at anything you do. You can perform at an improved level in sports, academics, or music with improved attention. You will do better on tests as a result of it. We usually do better when we have the capacity to focus on what we are doing, right?

But, there is more.

When you are unhappy, angry, or annoyed, paying attention to what is going on around you might assist you in calming down. You may be joyful and feel good with mindfulness, and it also helps you deal with difficult emotions.

Do you want to give mindfulness a try? I would!

Simple Mindfulness Exercises

- **Conscious Breathing**

  This is a great start if you want to practice mindfulness. Take a deep breath to begin. Here are some breathing techniques listed:

  ➤ **Hot Air Balloon**
    1. Cup your hand around your mouth.
    2. Take a deep breath with your nose and slowly blow out through your lips. As you do this, slowly extend your hands outward to mimic the expansion of a large bubble or hot air balloon.
    3. Repeat.
  ➤ **Animal Breaths**
    These animal breathing exercises may be the finest ones for your child to do if they enjoy

animals. Here are some of our favorite animal breathing methods, along with instructions on how to use them:

- o **Bunny Breathing:** Breath in through the nose three times quickly, then let out through the nose once more. Every time your kid performs this deliberate breathing exercise, have them practice slowing down the exhale.

- o **Snake Breathing:** Breath in via the nose for three seconds, hold the air for one second, then exhale while imitating a snake by hissing.

- o **Bumblebee Breathing:** The bumblebee breath is a variation of the bunny breath that likewise calls for using only your nose to inhale and exhale. However, regarding animal noises, this deep breathing method is comparable to snake breath. Instruct your youngster to imitate a bee by humming or buzzing when they exhale.

- **Noticing Sounds**

Go to a music class or play a kids' music video on the internet.

Listen to the sounds that are playing around you.

You can pick one and concentrate on it.

You can also listen to every sound and observe the drumbeat, bass line, and overall tempo.

Now play a kid's song and listen to the lyrics. You may have heard it innumerable times, and it may be one of your favorite tunes. This music may sound completely different to you if you listen to it mindfully.

- **Conscious Eating**

  Eat without engaging in any other activity. Choose the meal or food that you want to eat.

  Notice:

  - Feeling in your hands.
  - Its warmth, smell, flavor, and texture.
  - Determine the food's size and color.
  - Chew mindfully and slowly. Feel your attention shifting to the whole eating experience.

- **Conscious Movement**

  For this activity, you need to walk. It could be inside or outside. Below are some ideas for you to concentrate on:

  - Your joint muscles.
  - The sound of your feet contacting the floor or the ground.
  - Possibly an increase in pulse rate or some perspiration.
  - Once you have gotten the feel, add some playfulness to change things up. For instance, if you are outside, turn whenever you see a specific object (mailbox, blue car, etc.). You will become more present as a result of this.

- **Be Kind to Others**
  1. Sit and have deep breaths.

2. Think of someone and send your best wishes.
3. Wish for them to be pain-free.
4. Imagine them to be joyful, smiling, and laughing.

Mindfulness Exercises to Practice Anywhere

➢ **Stop**

This exercise will help you calm down. Here you go:

1. Stop.
2. Take deep breath.
3. Keep an eye on your emotions and thoughts.
4. Continue what you were doing before you paused but did so with more awareness and mindfulness.

➢ **RAIN**

Parents can discuss this activity with you and help you practice.

➢ **R for Recognize**

Recognize any powerful emotions you may be experiencing for a minute, then turn softly and openly toward them without passing judgement.

Pay attention to the emotions, ideas, and sensations that are present in your body and mind at the present moment.

Giving a name to it, such as "I'm feeling anxious" or "I'm feeling overwhelmed," might be useful. By acknowledging how you feel, you create an inner space where you may fully connect with yourself and the present reality.

➢ A for Allow

To "leave it be as it is" is to allow. It is the recognition and acceptance of the reality you are experiencing right now.

We do not have to like the circumstance in order to allow it to be. This is crucial because we frequently have an irrational urge to push aside, repress, or ignore challenging feelings. These kinds of inner conflicts unwittingly increase anguish and stress inside us.

We frequently become "caught up" in our thoughts and emotions during this unconscious battle, making it more probable that we will react instead of making a conscious decision.

We may bring an inner "yes" to our present-moment experience via letting or allowing. You could experience a softening and relaxation around the emotion almost instantly.

➢ I for Investigate

You have the choice to investigate this feeling now that you have acknowledged it and let it. You might not always feel like investigating is necessary; sometimes, just acknowledging and accepting yourself is enough. Other times, you might feel compelled to use this step naturally.

In order to research, you might ask yourself questions such as, "Why do I feel the way I do?" Are there any earlier incidents that might have affected the emotion? Is the feeling being influenced by physiological reasons (such as not getting enough sleep)? "What do I actually need at this moment?" What steps might I take to care for and assist others—or myself—during this trying time?

These questions can assist us in developing more mature relationships with our feelings and thoughts.

> **N for Non-Identification**

You focus on the straightforward knowledge that YOU are not your mind or your emotions in the "N" stage of R.A.I.N. You are the consciousness that permeates all thoughts, feelings, and sensory perceptions.

- **Body Scan**

Use your breath to direct your attention to every square inch of your body for this exercise. Continue to breathe as you feel your body from your head to your toes.

- **Surfing**

This practice might be extremely helpful when battling any stressed behavior. When you feel stressed over something:

> Recognize it and accept that you can feel it.
> Decide where you are feeling it.
> Do nothing except breathing deeply and slowly, both in and out.
> Keep your focus and breathing even when the desires rise and fall.

- **Narrow Your Attention**

Reducing anxiety and stress are perhaps the easiest and most essential mindfulness technique.

Locate a subject to observe. Study it as if you were going to take an exam on this item. Learn every detail about it. Give your attention to it so completely that nothing else, including stress, can enter your thoughts.

Chapter 3: Nourish Positive Thinking

A mental attitude known as positive thinking helps people see things more positively. It does not imply putting the bad behind us. Instead, a positive thinker recognizes a circumstance and approaches it in a useful way.

Positive thinking is an intrinsic ability due in part to brain changes that occur around middle childhood. Basic explanations of how emotions function are presented to us early in life, such as, "If I attend a birthday celebration, I will be happy. I will be sad if I get an injection." These principles persist through middle childhood and become more sophisticated beyond age five. Children need to comprehend that a person's ideas may affect how they feel, but their reality is independent of their thoughts.

Children may overcome problems in life by maintaining an optimistic outlook on things. A youngster who thinks positively will learn to approach many elements of life with optimism and be able to solve issues quickly. Children may experience negative effects from a small setback, but they should realize that does not spell the end of the world. They will be able to rapidly recover from challenging events if they maintain their optimism during them. Children who are positive tend to be more resilient. You should not make your kids ignore their bad thoughts or feelings; instead, encourage them to work through them and move on.

Here are some stories for you about positive attitudes.

Eagle or Chicken?

An eagle's egg once got confused with a hen's egg. The eagle's baby was one of the chickens that hatched from those eggs a few days later. They started growing up with them.

Like the other chicks, he would play about in the dirt wherever he pleased and eat the same thing all day long. He could fly a little higher than the other chicks and land with flailing wings.

Then one day, he witnessed an eagle flying confidently in the open sky. He asked the other chicks, "Who is that amazing bird soaring high?" "You cannot fly like that because you are a chicken!" they replied. The eagle child saw this reality and never made an effort to fly. He spent his entire life acting like chicks on the ground all because of his negative attitude. Even though he was born to fly high, he thought he could not and never even tried to do that.

Happy Fisherman

A fisherman used to sit by the water's edge of nature, watching under the shade of a tree. A wealthy businessman approached him and asked why he was sitting idle beneath a tree. The poor fisherman responded by saying that he had enough fish for the day.

When the wealthy guy heard this, he became enraged and asked: "Why do you not catch more fish instead of sitting in the shadows and wasting your time?"

The fisherman questioned, "What would I do if I caught more fish?"

The businessman replied assertively, "You could catch more fish, sell them, and make more money, all while purchasing a larger boat."

"What would I do then?" inquired the fisherman.

The businessman replied, "You could go deep-sea fishing to capture more fish and make more money."

"What would I do then?" inquired the fisherman.

The businessman argued, "You may purchase a large number of boats and hire a large number of workers to increase your income."

The conversation continued like this:

"What would I do then?

"You may achieve my level of wealth, businessman.

"What would I do then?"

"At that point, you may live in peace."

"What do you suppose I'm doing right now?" replied the fisherman.

When you think positively, you learn to be happy and content in the present, whatever that may be.

Discuss these stories with your parents. Now let's have some activities on positive thinking!

Activity: Impulse Control

During stressful events, we usually lose control and cannot figure out what is positive and negative. Below is a worksheet to help you identify positive and negative actions. Think of some stressful situations from your past life and write down what you did and think were positive or negative.

Impulse Control Activity

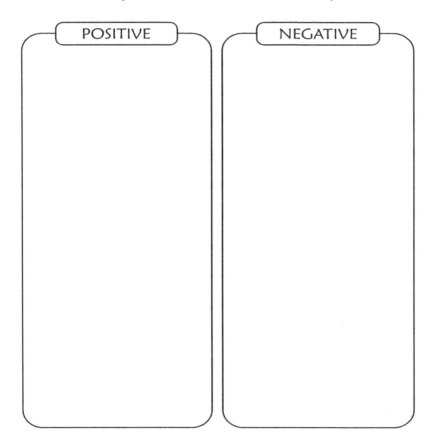

Activity: Negative Thoughts

Now here is a situation I have given you. Can you help John to deal with his negative thoughts?

Negative Thoughts

It is john's first day at his new school. He is having negative thoughts that are making him feel anxious. Can you help him change his thoughts?

I don't have any friends here. No one is going to like me.

My friends at my old school are having fun without me.

I'm so nervous. The kids will probably think that I'm weired.

This school is so big. I know for sure that I'm going to get lost.

Activity: My Choice: Ignore or Listen

Now, you are familiar with negative and positive thoughts and actions. Consider some stressful situations and write thoughts you had at that time. Write down your choice if you had to listen or ignore it.

SITUATION	Thoughts	MY CHOICE (Ignore/Listen)

Activity: Changing Thoughts

Change your daily negative thoughts into positive ones.

Changing Thoughts

What are some negative thoughts that you are having about a situation? What are some positive thoughts you can have instead?

Activity: Voice of Truth

Can you identify the voice of truth behind your negative thoughts? Write down the situation, your thoughts before the situation happened, and the truth when the situation passed.

SITUATION	WHAT WERE YOUR THOUGHTS	WHAT WAS TRUTH
Example: I need to solve a question and do not know how to solve it.	If I asked this question, the teacher would scold me.	I pushed myself to ask questions, and the teacher helped me to solve them.

Activity: Letting Go

Before negative thoughts disturb your peace of mind, learn to let go.

Letting....Go!

What are some anxious thoughts that you might need to let go?

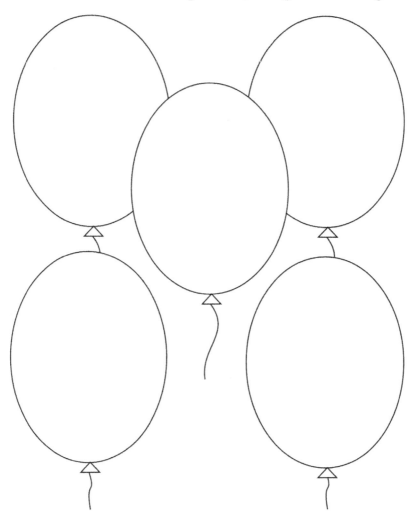

Activity: Flexible Thinking

Flexible Thinking Activity

Here is what to think about before starting a new task:

- Stop what I am doing

- What do I need to do?
- Do I have a checklist that I can use?

- Plan the steps needed to finish the task.
- Fit out the checklist that I can use

- Sit down and start working!

Activity: Think Sheet

Set some rules for yourself to help yourself deal with situations in a more positive light.

THINK SHEET

What rule did I break? _____

_____

_____

This means I was not: ☐ Being respectful
                       ☐ Being responsible
                       ☐ Following drections
                       ☐ Being kind
                       ☐ Being safe

My actions make me feel:

| happy | angry | confuesd | embarrassed | shocked | sad |

A different emotion? _____

I will fix my poor choice by: _____

_____

_____

Activity: The Voices in My Head

Now figure out what the voices in your head are saying to you. Whether they are positive or negative, talk to yourself positively and draw a picture that comes to your mind when you talk this way.

What are the voices in My Head Saying?

Negative Self - Talk	Positive Self - Talk
What thoughts stop me from doing my best? _____ _____ _____ _____	What thoughts keep me going so I can do my best? _____ _____ _____ _____

Draw a picture of you using your positive self - talk.

Activity: Crush All-or-Nothing Thinking

Use this worksheet to crush all negative thoughts.

HOW TO CRUSH
ALL - OR - NOTHING THINKING

Describe the situation.

(Current) Thoughts, Emotions, Actions	**(New)** Thoughts, Emotions, Actions
Capture the stories you tell.	What thoughts would create the new emotions?
Pinpoint the emotions your story triggers.	What emotion would drive the desired action?
Describe the result of your thoughts and emotions.	What is your desired action?

Activity: Thoughts Record Worksheet

Record your daily thoughts so that you can analyze your progress.

DAY	FEELINGS	THOUGHTS
MONDAY	Worry	I have a Math test today, and I think I will not be able to solve all the questions correctly.

Activity: What I Can/Cannot Control

Sometimes, we cannot control everything that we want to. So, here is an activity for you to think about all the things you can control and cannot. Write down in the drawing below and use red color for the things you cannot control. Select the other color of your choice.

What I Can/Can't Control

Write what you can control inside the body and write what you can't control outside of the body. Remember: you can only control your actions.

Chapter 4: Self-Regulation Fun Activities

The ability to control oneself is essential for kids. Instead of only acting on our impulses, this capacity enables us to regulate our behavior and make wise judgments over the long run. We can also control our emotions, whether we are furious, upset, or anxious, due to this ability. These emotions can be demanding for adults, but for children and young people, whose brains are still growing and developing, they are substantially more difficult.

The benefits of assisting children and teenagers in developing their self-regulation abilities are enormous. These abilities can support children and young adults in a variety of ways, including helping them finish their work and chores (even if they do not want to), keep their friendships strong, make safe decisions while out with friends, stop themselves from breaking the law, persevere through obstacles when they feel like giving up, and much more.

The parent-child relationship is stressed by a youngster who struggles to control their emotions. This might have a detrimental domino effect on the entire family, including siblings or others close to them, and cause a downward cycle. Similar to friendships, children who cannot manage their strong emotions have the less social capability. They find it more difficult to make and maintain friendships. Big emotions that are difficult to control might manifest in features like rage, withdrawal, anxiety, or violent conduct.

All of these might have further detrimental effects: Children who experience peer rejection are more likely to struggle with school dropout, criminality, drug misuse, and antisocial conduct. Bullying is more likely to occur in people who are isolated and rejected by their peers.

When we are unable to regulate and manage our emotions, thoughts and behavior, every situation becomes stressful. So let's help you develop self-regulation skills.

4.1 Fun Games for Self-Regulation

Here are top self-control games to get you started for self-regulation:

- **The Freeze Dance**

    Have a dance party with a small group of children or family members, and instruct everyone to hold still when the music is turned off. The first one to move is disqualified from continuing to the next round. The last dancer standing wins.

- **Traffic Lights**

    In this game, one child turns towards a wall while acting as a traffic cop. The other children stand on the other side of the room or at a starting line if they are outside. The children can move forward when the traffic cop calls, "Green!" When a traffic cop yells "Red!" the children are required to stop, and the officer gets to turn around and observe if everyone complies. Any child who is still moving can be sent back to the starting line if they are caught. The winner is the first kid to cross the courtyard or room.

- **Musical Chairs**

  Place enough chairs in a row, facing front and back alternately, for each player, minus one. Kids can dance or walk around the chairs while music is played. They must rush to the nearest chair as soon as the music ends and sit on it. The kid unable to secure a chair is eliminated in every round until only one victorious player is left.

- **Musicians**

  Give your friends acoustic instruments to play, and instruct them to follow a child standing in the front acting as a conductor and holding a baton. Everyone must adjust their speed and slow down by the conductor's prescribed tempo. They will learn to coordinate their body motions to produce an amazing sound.

- **Jenga**

  This stacking game needs a steady hand and quick thinking. Stack up the Jenga tower blocks into a tower and remove the blocks from the tower one by one, not letting the tower fall. How tall can you make your tower? Can you stack the blocks by using horizontal and vertical ways both? Use your imagination.

4.2 Fun Activities for Self-Regulation

Here are some activities to help you self-regulate your emotions.

- **Pay it Forward**

  Acting kindly or compassionately toward the other

person or animal is known as paying it forward. People frequently discover that helping others makes them happy. You should practice being kind when you experience sadness, loneliness, anger, or when anyone needs to be cheered up.

You only need paper, a pencil or pen, and your intellect to practice paying it forward! The first step is to consider any individuals or animals that could use some assistance. Then, you can think of ways you could be of assistance. Some concepts are:

> Giving a younger sibling, cousin, or friend a book to read.
> Supplying a food bank with food.
> Removing rubbish from the beach or your community.
> Volunteering at a shelter for animals.
> Assisting neighbors or family members with their yard.
> Offering to watch a youngster for a family member.
> Bringing a treat or snack to a sick person.
> Giving a buddy or classmate a compliment.
> Making cards for children who are hospitalized or attending school.

You will discover quickly that giving to others makes you feel wonderful too!

- **Directed Imagery**

Through the use of guided imagery, you may concentrate on a pleasant scene or image in your mind.

It is a tool you always have with you since you can do it whenever and wherever you are. Particularly for kids who are still learning about emotions and how the mind functions, guided imagery offers several advantages. It facilitates stress and anxiety reduction and promotes physical and mental relaxation. Children have the ability to focus on one picture that they associate with positively while letting other ideas flow through their brains through guided imagery exercises. This exercise is especially beneficial for kids who are easily overstimulated and require techniques for slowing down and consuming fewer stimuli.

Explain the benefits of guided imagery by stating that it is a technique for creating mental images that can promote calmness and relaxation. Next, walk them through this straightforward guided visualization exercise.

> ➢ Find a comfortable position. Sit or lie down as you like. Take note of how your mind and body feel like.
> ➢ Breathe in deeply through your nose, and then exhale through your mouth.
> ➢ Take another breath. As you exhale, feel the calmness spreading throughout your entire body.
> ➢ Breathe deeply and gently like you always do.
> ➢ Inhale calmly, and exhale whatever problems you may have. Breathe in, and release all your worries as you exhale.

- Now picture in your mind a location where you are completely at ease and content. This may be a favorite location that you have visited, a location that you have seen, or it may be entirely fictitious. You have the choice.
- Imagine a peaceful and happy place.
- Now, begin to include details: What can you see there? Do you hear anything? What smell fills this wonderful, peaceful, happy place?
- Consider how your body is feeling. You are calm and content, enjoying the pleasant weather, and delighted to be performing whatever delightful things you choose to do in this place.
- Enjoy how safe you feel in this setting.
- Keep sitting as you practice being at ease and comfortable.
- Take note of your environment once again at this place. Take a few seconds to simply breathe and take it all in. It will soon be time to depart, but remember that you may come back here whenever you want in your mind to unwind, feel at ease, and feel safe and secure.
- I will start counting to three in a moment. On the count of three, you can awake and revitalize yourself. First, inhale deeply, and then gently exhale.
- Two... exhale after taking a second big breath...
- Three... you are feeling confident, calm, and refreshed.

- **Expressing Gratitude**

  It is not necessary to wait until Thanksgiving to express gratitude. It is a practice that can be carried out at any time, whether morning, afternoon or evening. It is a fun method to help you gain perspective and elevate your mood.

  Being grateful can be incredibly beneficial when one is worried, cranky, frustrated, unhappy, or angry. It can also help one remember the wonderful things in their lives when feeling great.

  To express gratitude, list the things you are grateful for, such as your house and possessions, past experiences, or the people in your life. You can then record gratitude in a journal or notepad and embellish it with stickers, drawings, or other scrapbooking tools.

  Here are some additional methods to practice gratitude besides making a list:

  > Send a letter to a loved one. Explain why you like them. The letter can be delivered in person, over the phone, or mailed to them.
  > Note down three positive things that happened to you each day for a week. Examples can be that you made a new friend, did well on an exam or had a fantastic chat with a friend.
  > In addition to the three positive events, write about what led to the positive event or why it occurred. Did you try a new hobby or make a

new colleague by saying hello, for instance? Did you perform well on a test because you were an expert in the subject or because of your extensive preparation?

➤ Send someone your best wishes. Give the person your list of all the good things you want them to have. Pick two persons to send encouraging thoughts to a close relative, such as a sibling or grandparent, and a more distant relative or acquaintance.

Enjoy offering thanks while watching how it might help you decompress!

- **Journaling**

You can record your everyday activities and express your feelings and thoughts in a notebook. You can use it to reduce stress, discover more about yourself, deal with intense emotions, and find solutions to issues. There is no incorrect way to journal. It can be beneficial when someone is anxious, afraid, or furious, as well as when they are enthusiastic about something.

Find a notepad and a pen to get started. Although typing on a computer or tablet is good, pen and paper are still the best options. The ideal environment for journaling is peaceful, calm, and free from distractions.

Start writing or typing! Here are some topics to assist you in getting started if you struggle with writing. You may write regarding:

➤ Your actions today

> What is you thinking and why?
> Something about which you are concerned and why
> When you were confident or strong today
> Something about your current situation in life that you would change

A journal can be kept privately by an individual or shared with others. Starting with 10 to 15 minutes of journaling is a good idea. The more you write in a journal, the more you discover and feel good about yourself.

4.3 Group Exercises

Here are ten enjoyable group activities for practicing and learning self-control that do not need any setup or special equipment:

- **Mother, May I?**

  Kids, if you have never played this game before, it is a good idea to take turns playing the lead of "mother" and leading the game's action.

  The Mother, May I Game rules are as follows:
  > Each player should be positioned with their shoulders approximately a foot apart.
  > In front of the other players, the player who is "Mother" should stand.
  > The mother then addresses a specific child by name and provides them with instructions so they may proceed. "Emma, take 2 GIANT steps forward," for instance.

- ➢ The next command is for the called-up youngster to say, "Mother, May I?"
- ➢ Mother then answers with either a "Yes" or a "No," after which the kid might move ahead or remain still.
- ➢ A youngster who moves but does not say, "Mother, May I?" must start over at the beginning.
- ➢ If another youngster walks the steps before their turn, they too must return to the beginning point.
- ➢ The youngster who gets to Mother first wins!

- **Simon Says**

  Children participating in the Simon Says game must only act when the leader says, "Simon Says do..." For instance, if the leader says, "Simon Says touch your toes," every child does so. No one is allowed to move if the commander instructs them not to.

- **Body Part Mix Up**

  The leader will call out different body parts for the kids to touch in the "Body Part Mix Up." For instance, when the leader yells "knees," the kids touch their knees, but in this game, you should make rules for interchanging the body part names. Touch your toes each time the leader says, "Head," rather than your head. The kids must pause, consider their behaviors, and refrain from simply reacting. The leader can even yell three body part names at once, like "Knees, head, elbow!" To change up the game, add new rules.

- **Follow the Leader**

  The kids must mimic the leader's actions. Everyone

  wobbles in response to the leader's command, "Ready, Set, Wiggle." " Ready, Set, Watermelon!" the leader yells. Nobody needs to move. The leader yells, "Ready...Set...Wigs!" No one will move. The leader shouts, "Ready...Set...Wiggle." Once more, everyone wiggles. You are free to modify this sentence any way you want. The idea is to have the kids wait to move until a specific word is spoken aloud.

- **Color Moves**

  Inform all the group members that they will move around the space. They are to move depending on the color of the paper the leader is holding up. The yellow paper indicates a regular walking pace, while the blue paper indicates a slow pace. They stop if the leader holds up a red piece of paper. Try out various locomotor activities, such as marching, jumping, and stationary running.

Kids, I hope these activities and games will keep you active and entertained, all the while learning important self-regulation skills.

Chapter 5: Self-Regulation through Relaxation Exercises

Humans might not be able to regulate their emotions completely, but contrary to popular belief, they can develop a lot of control over how they feel. Learning the techniques to feel better through better emotional management does not cost a fortune or money. These techniques are known as emotion regulation abilities (see self-regulation in chapter 4), allowing you to control and influence your emotions.

This chapter will teach you how to control your emotions and assist you in honing the abilities required to maintain emotional stability and balance through relaxation exercises.

Let's go through these research-based fun exercises.

5.1 Breathing Exercises

Children are given a lifelong tool for a strong sense of self when they become aware of how they are breathing and how to adjust and manage their breath on their own.

Hi Kids! Are you excited?

- **Rubber Breath**

  This mindfulness exercise is so entertaining for calming, focusing, and soothing; it is like giving yourself a big hug. It is a fantastic tool every time you need to start something new or challenging.

Additionally, it is effective when you feel agitated, frustrated, or overburdened.

> ➢ Put one hand on the belly. It needs to be just above your belly button.

> ➢ Put your other hand on the center of your chest where your sternum is. Let your parents show you where the sternum bone is. It is a long flat bone in the middle of your chest.

> ➢ Breathe deeply thrice and hum as you exhale. As you hum, let the vibration energize your body and ease your worries.

- **Abdomen Breathing**

Your respiration, heartbeat, and muscle tension may all rise when you are anxious or stressed, making it more difficult to think effectively. However, when you can calm their bodies down through techniques like belly breathing, it helps lessen your pain and worry.

How can you learn belly breathing?

> ➢ First, sit or lie down with your legs on the floor.

> ➢ Put a hand on the chest and another on the belly.

> ➢ Encourage yourself to inhale deeply and fill your lungs with air.

> ➢ As you take a breath in, your tummy gets big. Keep the hand on your chest still.

> Blow all the air out while making the shape like the letter "O" with your lips.

> As muscles contract, you should feel your stomach flatten.

You can practice belly breathing if you need to unwind or are in discomfort. The more you practice belly breathing, the better you will get at it, just as with any other ability.

- **Fish Breathing**

Fish breathing exercise is an enjoyable practice because you make a fish-like bloop sound when you exhale. I am sure you will end up laughing, a useful approach to release tension and encourage yourself not to take life too seriously.

According to physiological principles, when you breathe deeply, you take in a lot of oxygen, which your body and brain require to be calm and awake. You can breathe more oxygen when you expel carbon dioxide since greater oxygen allows us to relax and recharge.

> Inhale deeply through your nose.

> Expand your cheeks and...

> Force the air through your lips...

> Bloooooooop, blooooooooop, bloop, bloop.

> Take another big breath through your nose.

> Open your mouth and exhale.

> Bloooooooop, blooooooooop, bloop, bloop.

- **Balloon Breathing**

   Practice balloon breathing by following these steps:

   > Take a long, deep breath using your nose.

   > Next, let out a little hissing sound via your mouth, like a balloon gradually losing air or a snake hissing.

   > Try to extend the exhale to at least 15 seconds extremely slowly.

   > Hiss while slowing their inner speed.

Repetition of these breathing exercises can help kids understand how to use their breath to mentally and physically slow down.

5.2 Mindfulness Coloring

Use the coloring charts on the next page to practice mindfulness. Whenever you feel stressed or down, you can use these sheets to brighten up your mood through coloring.

5.3 Yoga Poses

Everyone may benefit from yoga, and getting started while you are young can work wonders since it builds a strong foundation for your health. You reside in a world that moves quickly today. You continually take in information from everything around you and start to feel a variety of societal and personal stresses. You need coping mechanisms that yoga can provide if you are going to handle these challenges properly. They develop a strong and resourceful body, mind, and soul via yoga practice. Children who practice yoga are reported to have more intimate relationships with both themselves and their surroundings. As a result, individuals can control their emotions, lower their stress levels, and become calmer and more present.

So let's start with simple yoga positions like these:

- **Cow and Cat Pose**

    ➢ Position yourself on the floor like a cow or a cat.

    ➢ Inhale and look up while arching your back.

    ➢ Exhale as you tuck your tailbone and bring your chin to your chest.

    ➢ Repeat at least five times more.

- **Butterfly Position**

    ➢ Extend your legs in the direction of your chest while sitting down on the ground.

> Then, with the knees out to the sides, bring the heels of the feet together.

> Grab your shins or ankles.

> Maintain this position for at least five breath cycles.

- **Puppy Pose**

> Get down on your hands and feet and begin.

> Then, slowly raise your hips to the sky while lifting your knees in the shape of an upside-down letter V.

> For at least three breaths, hold the puppy pose.

- **Branch Pose**

> Position your feet shoulder-width apart as you stand.

> Put the left foot under your lower leg or shin while shifting your weight to the right leg.

> Bring your hands up toward the sky as though they were tree branches.

> Continue on the other leg after being in this position for a few breath cycles.

Use the yoga art therapy worksheet on the next page to try more poses.

Yoga Art Therapy

Learn It:	Draw It:	Do It:
Strength		
Calm		
Brave		
Peaceful		
Wise		

5.4 Muscle Relaxation Technique

The best technique to help children whose bodies or brains are anxious, tense, or unhappy is to relax their muscles. It enables the mind to settle down and concentrate just on that subject by tensing and relaxing various muscles. Additionally, it can assist both children and adults in learning to identify when stress or concern may produce discomfort and tightness in various regions of their bodies and how to release it.

Kids, you should settle into a relaxed place before beginning to practice muscle relaxation. You may have your feet on the floor when lying down or sitting in a chair. Then exhale five to ten times from the belly. Then, concentrate on relaxing and tensing the various body parts. Read the instructions below for the various body parts:

<u>Face</u>: Start by tightening every muscle in your face, including the ones in the eyes, cheeks, nose, and forehead. Put your hands on your face. Hold firmly and count to ten. The muscle in your face will then relax as you release the tension.

<u>Hands</u>: Tense up your fists and visualize yourself squeezing something hard in your hands, such as lemons, to extract their juice.

<u>Jaw</u>: Begin with tensing your jaw by biting down as if you were holding a big ball in your mouth. Release after ten seconds of holding.

Move on to your **neck and shoulders**, pressing and raising your shoulders to your ears in the shape of a turtle. Just let go.

This can be done several times. Keep taking belly breaths with each exercise.

Arms: Stretch your arms upward until they feel like they can reach the ceiling, then release. Alternately, tighten your arms toward your body and hold for a little time before letting go.

Back: Attempt to press your shoulders together while arching your back; hold for a moment, and then release.

Move to your **belly**, sucking it in and hardening it like a rock. After three seconds, release it after holding it.

Legs, feet, and toes: Next, focus on your legs, feet, and toes. Squeeze, curl, and then release your toes under your feet. Imagine relaxing each of your muscles and experiencing a pleasant sense of warmth.

So kids, did you enjoy these exercises?

Chapter 6: Stress Buster Strategies

Not being able to manage stress is a growing issue in children. School, schoolwork, friends, family upheavals, habit changes, and various other conditions can cause stress, as we discussed at the beginning of the book. Stress might manifest physically in the form of tears or headaches, or it can manifest emotionally or behaviorally in the form of concern or shyness. The age and developmental stage of the child can influence how they respond to stress.

Early childhood professionals can intervene with stress-relieving techniques before minor stressors become major issues if they recognize stress in young children. Children can learn a variety of coping mechanisms to help them deal with stress in this chapter. In our fast-paced, hectic, and always-changing world, it is easy for kids to feel overwhelmed by worry and anxiety. Thus, the following strategies can help your kids handle stressful situations gracefully.

6.1 Lifestyle Strategies

Stress in young people does not always appear the same as stress in adults. But just like adults, kids and teenagers — even those who have had losses that have changed their lives — can learn appropriate coping mechanisms. Young people may learn to recognize the symptoms of excessive stress and, with the correct tools, manage it with the help of their parents or other caregivers.

Kids, here are some lifestyle strategies for you:

- Watch out for your sleep needs.

- Regular exercise can help you improve your focus and cognitive skills. Exercise for thirty minutes, five to six days a week, improves focus. Rest and exercise are crucial for your hormone and anxiety management.

  Moreover, going outside and being active might help your emotions balance if you feel bored, worn out, hyperactive, upset, angry, or anxious.

- Use essential oils to boost memory and reduce stress. The mental health media network claims that if you are exposed to the same smell when learning and resting, you will remember more of what you have learned. Keep a tiny bowl of essential oils beside your study desk or bed so you can observe its fragrance. For instance, peppermint oil can be utilized to relax the body.

You do not need a lot of time or resources to keep your mind and body active through exercises and activities. You can use your family's creativity as a resource for enjoyable activities. The options are unlimited once you get the go-ahead! You can engage in a familiar pastime or try something new.

Activities to Get Moving

For kids:

> A family outdoor stroll.

> Riding a bike or tricycle.

> Organizing and cleaning your space.

> Playing outside.

- Chasing after your pet.

- Swimming.

- Observing a fun, age-appropriate exercise video.

- Dancing to music you enjoy.

- Playing sports-related games with family and friends.

- Jumping rope.

- Playing catch or making 3-pointers.

Are you usually anxious around the time you have a test at school? Let me share my secrets with you.

Test Strategies

Cramming for an exam or quiz is not a good idea. This calls for a lot of work, overworking your brain, and no breaks during study time—all of which are more challenging for you if you are already stressed.

The best approach is "distributed practice," or studying for small periods across several days. You can make a schedule just for your work. The understanding and retention of information are both improved by sleep.

Motivate yourself to study for past exams or practice exams. This teaches you how to manage time and familiarize yourself with the paper's format.

Learn how to use various exam strategies, such as missing and coming back to problems when unsure of the answer or removing the multiple-choice answers you know are erroneous.

Before going to bed, review study materials by allowing yourself to digest information while sleeping; this technique improves memory.

If you wish for any special accommodations for the exam, such as the ability to sit in a location with the lowest distractions possible, get in touch with the teacher.

6.2 Emotional Strategies

Express your opinions on what troubles you. You can even just share it with your diary. Although talking to someone about your stress issues can be helpful, a University of Chicago study discovered that twenty minutes of writing and reading (about the stress) could help to lessen symptoms. This helps to control excessive overthought and negative thoughts.

Reframe your self-defeating thoughts. You may think, "I never get good grades," or "I won't pass this test." Self-talk is a component of cognitive-behavioral therapy (CBT) and effectively improves stress symptoms. Use positive statements like, "I'm prepared, and I will accomplish all I can." In addition to reducing stress, it also fosters self-confidence.

Reframe feelings of anxiety. Tell yourself that physical sensations like sweaty palms, a rapid heartbeat, or stomach "butterflies" might help me think more clearly and argue more persuasively. This can assist you in maintaining composure and help you manage your emotions.

Envision "perfect (exam/...) day." Learn relaxation strategies you can employ throughout the (exam/...) if anxiety symptoms appear, such as deep breathing, muscle relaxation, guided imagery etc.

I hope these strategies will help you work on the triggers for stress.

THE END NOTE

Children nowadays experience higher levels of stress, anxiety, and depression than children in earlier generations, whether it is due to constant access to technology, a busier schedule than ever before, or other factors. Younger grade-schoolers might be unable to properly comprehend or articulate their feelings related to childhood stress. That is why they need your help. It will be easier if you help them solve issues before they negatively affect you if you are aware of changes in your behavior.

Working as a family to detect stress and discover coping mechanisms is crucial. Parents should ask their child how they are regularly doing and listen. Children need to know that their parents are there for them. As soon as you pinpoint the sources of your stress—such as excessive homework, too many extracurricular activities, or cyberbullying—you may work with them to find solutions. You might need to leave a challenging class or cut back on your involvement in extracurricular activities. You might also need to use social media more wisely and how to unplug from technology.

Additionally, parents should educate their kids about proactive stress reduction techniques. These tactics might consist of making the child's room cold, dark, quiet, and screen-free, which will help them sleep better, stretching, deep breathing, meditation, or physical activity into their daily routine to calm their anxiousness.

It can also be allowing time in the schedule for self-care, such as recreation, reading, or other relaxing activities. It may do a lot for a child's mental health to give them time to just be themselves, free from social obligations, homework, or soccer practice.

Your children would not always see you as content and joyful. According to Smith, it is beneficial for kids to understand that stress, melancholy, frustration, and other unpleasant emotions are common and healthy parts of life. However, it is crucial to set a good example for their children by finding healthy methods to cope with stressful situations.

Stress also makes it simpler to develop bad family routines, such as ordering takeout because you lack the energy to prepare. Researchers have shown that children of parents who experience stress—whether it is due to health issues, financial difficulties, or other worries—eat fast food more frequently, engage in less physical activity, and are more likely to be fat.

When you do make an effort to relax, you might be tempted to pick unhealthy comforts like bingeing on ice cream or passing out in front of the TV. By seeing their parents, children can learn how to deal with stress.

The parent-child relationship is crucial no matter what intervention is used. Parents' continual support doubles the impact of children's self-regulatory skills, shared memories, and hours invested together doing daily things like reading a book, cooking, or dancing. These are, without question, the most powerful and long-lasting foundations for stress management.

Made in United States
North Haven, CT
23 February 2023